12 Grand Waltzes
for piano

by Grant Dersom

Copyright © 2019, 2021 Grant Dersom

All rights reserved. No part of this book or the music contained within may be duplicated or otherwise reproduced in any form or medium without physical written permission from the copyright holder.

ISBN: 978-1-7377719-0-6

Printing Epoch: 4

Published by Sonive Publishing

Visit www.sonive.com for more information.

Foreword

Starting off, I'd like to say thank you so much for your support—not only for your patronage, but also because it brings me a lot of joy just knowing someone else is hearing and playing this music.

I wrote this book as a simplified version of a larger book I published, titled "24 Waltzes." The original version has some pretty difficult moments, and at the recommendation of my friends, I decided to arrange the music from 12 of the more simplifiable waltzes to become the 12 Grand Waltzes. Because these waltzes originally come from that other book, you may notice that the waltz numbers "skip" around, from No. 1, to No. 3, to No. 5, etc.—this happens because they reflect their numbers in the collection of 24, not in this collection of 12.

In the next few pages, I have also included some performance notes to explain some of the book's more unclear markings. Don't worry about following everything to a "T"; the extra instructions are intended to help guide a deeper interpretation, though oftentimes the best interpretation flows from being thoroughly engaged in the piece you're playing rather than thrashing with the details.

Anyway, thank you again, and I hope you enjoy playing my music.

Grant Dersom

Performance Notes

accel. a tempo

This indicates that the tempo should be sped back up until it reaches the original tempo.

Fingerings

All fingerings are **suggestions**: play as you feel most comfortable.

Mordents

To clarify interpretation, I created two types of mordents: the early mordent and the late mordent. Early mordents start before the beat and finish on the beat, while late mordents start on the beat; the vertical line in the symbol represents the beat.

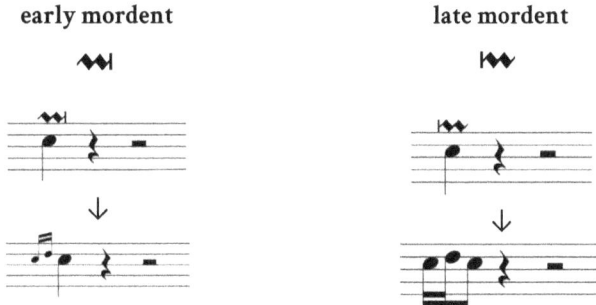

Octave marks (8va)

An 8va mark below the staff means play an octave lower, while an 8va mark above the staff means play an octave higher. (An 8va below the left hand means "8vb", or an octave lower.)

Pedaling

I use the damper and sustain pedals constantly, changing based on the musical situation. A *con pedale* mark in this music means that the pedal should be used throughout, ad lib. Some pieces also give specific instructions for pedaling for guidance purposes.

Straight lines

Lines connecting notes show where each voice continues throughout a more complicated section. They are not indicators of a slide; do not play notes between the connected notes.

Tenuto

Tenuto marks indicate that the section or note(s) around the mark should emphasized and played at a slower tempo.

All glory be to God.

Contents

Pg. 3 — 1.

Pg. 6 — 3.

Pg. 9 — 5.

Pg. 13 — 6.

Pg. 16 — 7.

Pg. 20 — 9.

Pg. 23 — 11.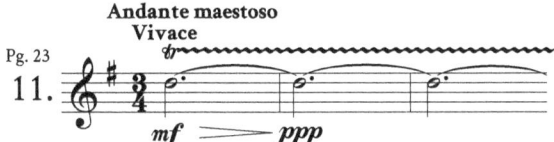

Pg. 26 — 12.

Pg. 30 — 16.

Pg. 33 — 17.

Pg. 38 — 18.

Pg. 43 — 24.

Waltz
in C major

Grant Dersom
February 10, 2018

Waltz No. 1

Waltz
in C minor

Grant Dersom
February 18, 2018

Waltz No. 3

* ending finger; mordent may be executed as 2 - 3 - 1, or 1 - 3 - 1, etc.

Waltz No. 3

WALTZ
in B minor

Grant Dersom
February 19-28, 2018

Waltz No. 5

Waltz No. 5

Waltz No. 5

WALTZ

in C sharp minor

Grant Dersom

February 21-March 1, 2018

Molto vivace

♩ = **195**, or as fast as possible

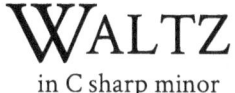

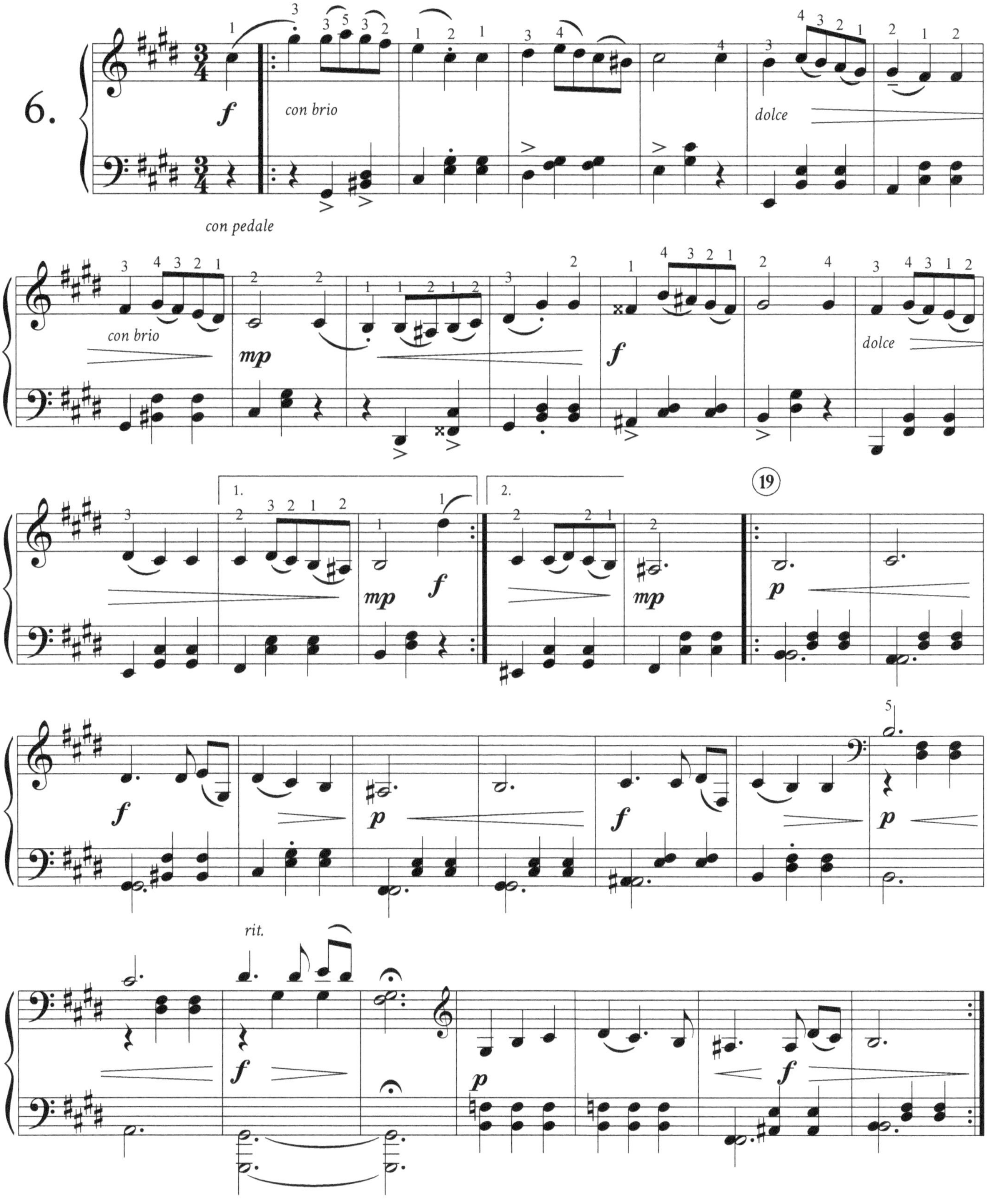

Waltz No. 6

Waltz
in E minor

Grant Dersom
March 16, 2018

Waltz No. 7

Waltz No. 7

Waltz
in A flat major

Grant Dersom
March 18, 2018

Waltz No. 9

Waltz
in G major

Grant Dersom
April 4, 2018

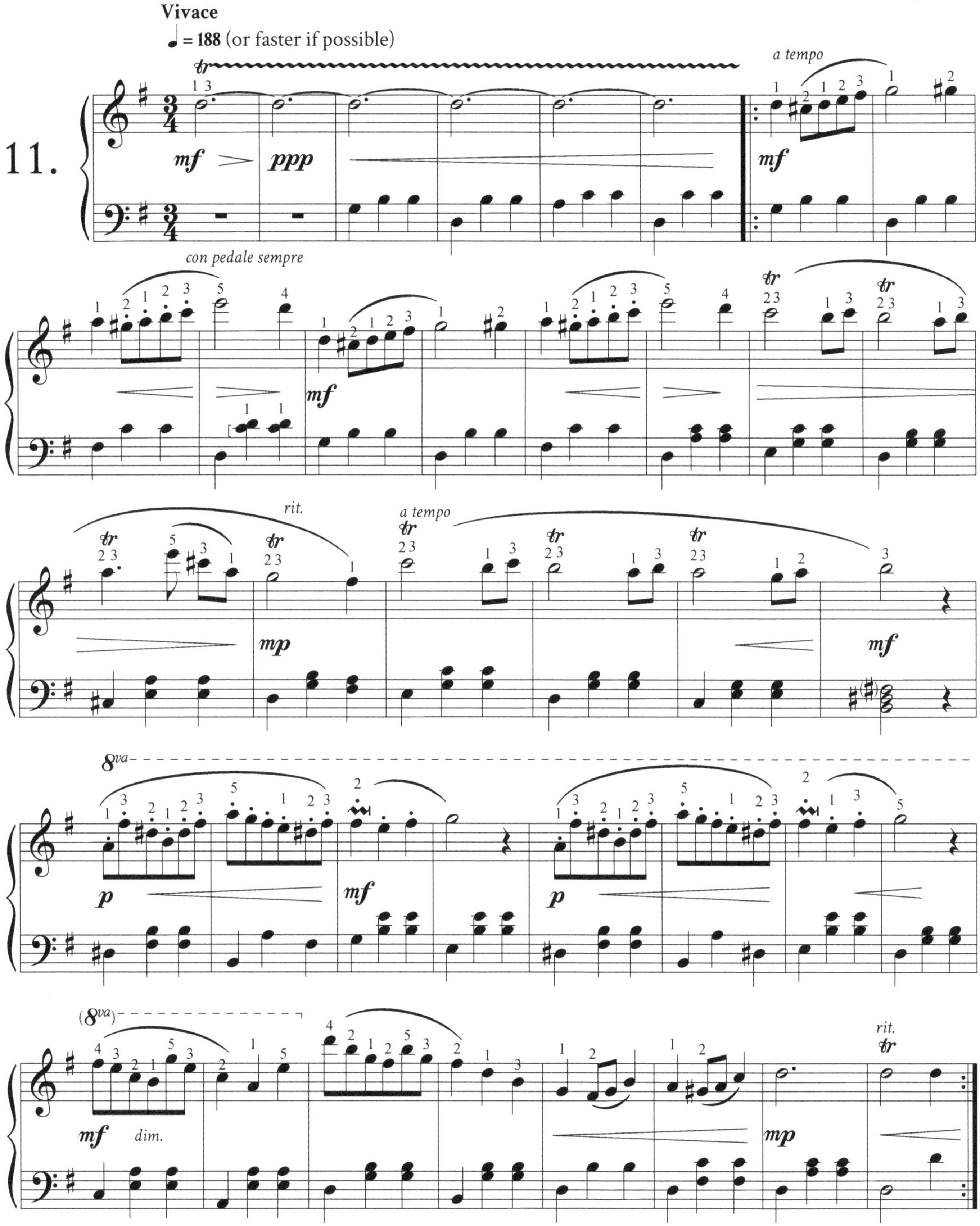

Vivace
♩ = **188** (or faster if possible)

Waltz No. 11

Waltz No. 11

Waltz
in E major

Grant Dersom
April 10, 2018

Waltz No. 12

Waltz No. 12

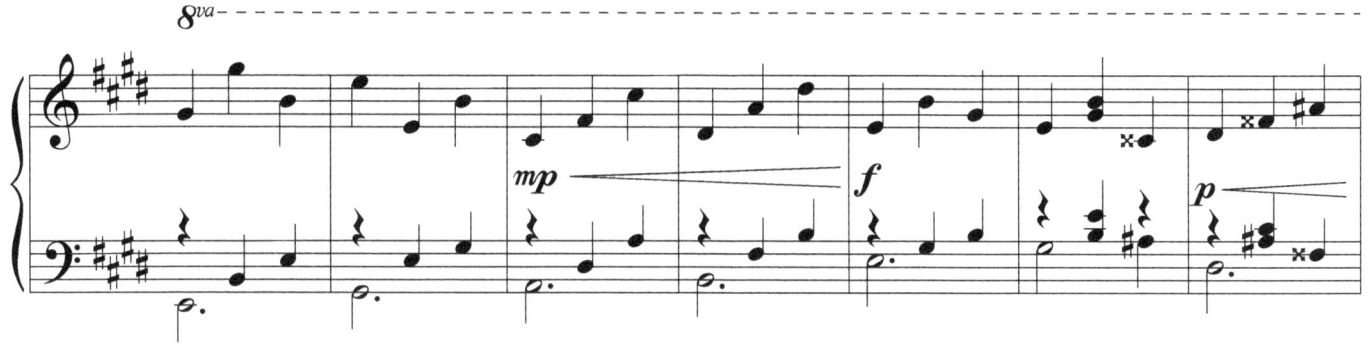

Waltz No. 12

Waltz
in E flat major

Grant Dersom
April 24, 2018

Waltz No. 16

Waltz No. 16

Waltz

in A minor

Grant Dersom
May 14, 2018

Moderato con brio

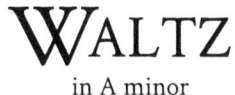

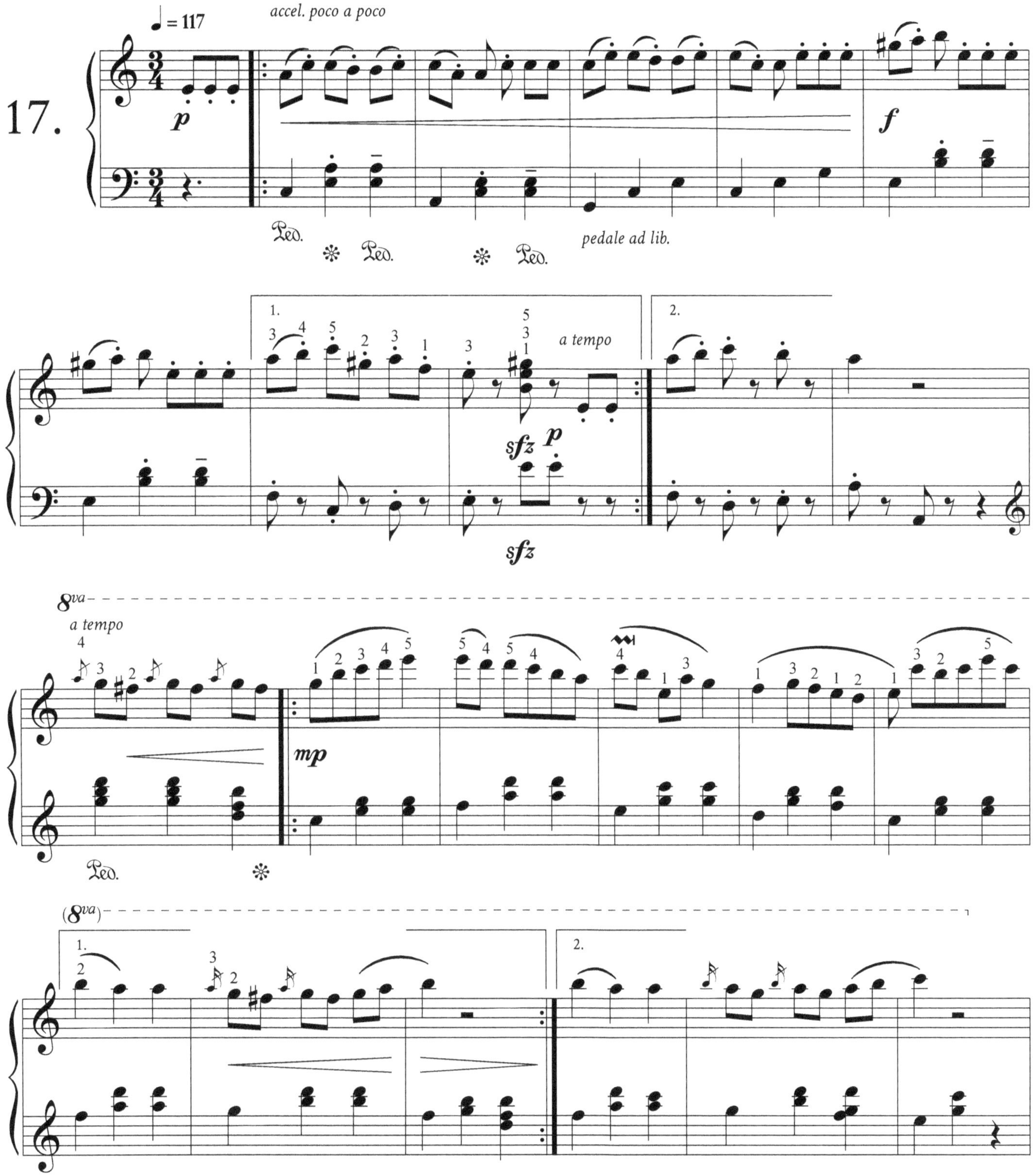

Waltz No. 17

Waltz No. 17

Waltz No. 17

Waltz No. 17

Waltz
in B flat major

Grant Dersom
May 2, 2018

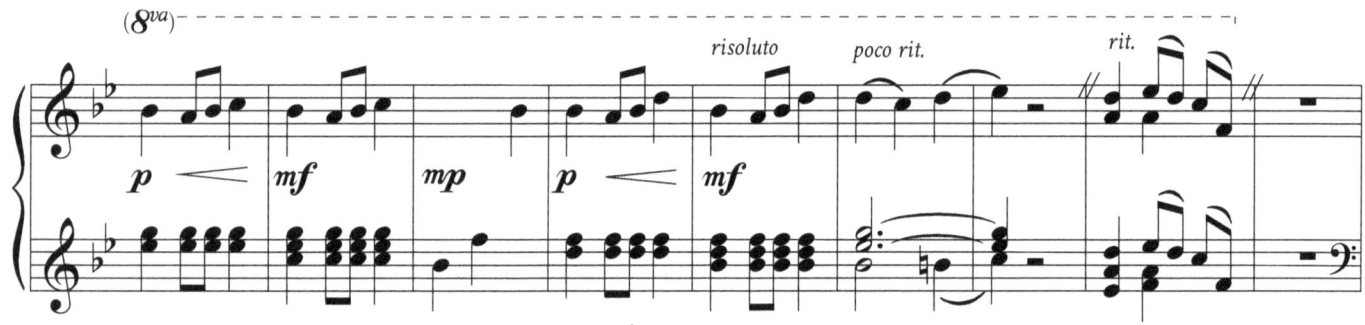

Waltz No. 18

Waltz No. 18

Waltz No. 18

Waltz No. 18

Waltz
in F major

Grant Dersom
July 6, 2018

Adagio maestoso e dolce

Waltz No. 24

Waltz No. 24

Waltz No. 24

47

Fine.

Waltz No. 24

Thank you!

Leave a review (if you want!)

We have more music at

sonive.com/music

Other books

Satie: 3 Gymnopédies
(Zero Page Turns Edition)

Original compositions

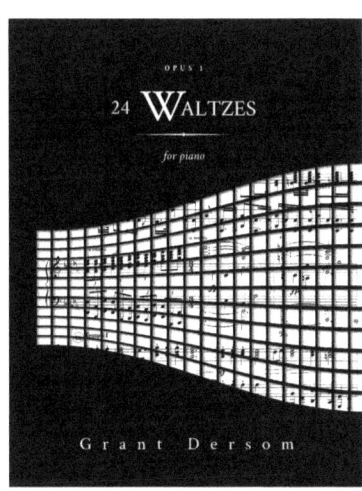

24 Waltzes, Op. 1

www.ingramcontent.com/pod-product-compliance
Lightning Source LLC
Chambersburg PA
CBHW051319110526
44590CB00031B/4405